Sex As . . .

A JOURNAL FOR YOUR LIFE

JEFF DEVORE

ISBN 978-1-956010-84-8 (paperback)
ISBN 978-1-956010-85-5 (digital)

Rushmore Press LLC
1 800 460 9188
www.rushmorepress.com

Printed in the United States of America

Table of Contents

Acknowledgements

Thank you.

To all who have loved and supported me as I crawled, crept, toddled, stumbled, walked, stumbled again, fell, got up, and continued;

To you who taught and mentored me;

To you who surrounded me with a family's love;

To you who trusted me as your chiropractor, as your pastor, as your coach;

To you who stayed by me, wrote to me, sent me books, took my calls during those years I was away;

To you who befriended me, housed me, employed me, counseled me, welcomed me into your home, into your heart, into your gatherings;

To you who believed in me when I could hardly believe in myself,

To you who caught the vision of this book, who gave helpful feedback and suggestions,

Thank you.

The light of your love brings sight, hope, warmth, healing and courage.

Your love softens defenses and nurtures life.

To you and to the Love who consistently and reliably surprises, comforts, enlightens, strengthens, and heals us when we relax, trust, and open ourselves, I say, "Thank You!"

Introduction

Welcome to the truth about sex.

Your truth.

Who else's truth is there?

Some people write books, poems, and plays about sex; others research it and publish the data, the findings, outcomes, and conclusions ("more research is warranted"); some make drawings or take photos; others shoot videos and movies; others scratch messages on bathroom walls or carve pictures and words into the trunk of a tree; others blog, sext and send tweets.

After all that, it remains . . .

You are the only person in the universe who has ever experienced sex in the ways that you have. The ONLY person.

This makes you the expert on your sex life.

You carry memories, current awareness, and fears, hopes and dreams (the past, the present, the future) of this swirling, boundless complexity we call sex. All that is stored in the cells and molecules of your body, some in neurons of your brain, some in glandular hormones, some in muscles and tissues waiting to rise to the occasion, some as a vibration of energy calling for expression.

You are invited, using the freedom and power of your expertise, to express your memories, awarenesses, fears, hopes, and dreams. Explore and exploit the pages of this journal.

Thumb through it.

Let a page call to you. Respond with a word, a sentence, a paragraph, a story, a poem. Sketch an image. Create a collage.

When finished, pick another page.

Then another.

Return to the first one you selected and jot or sketch some more.

Use the five pages at the end of the journal to choose your own words.

Be courageous. Express your truth.

If and when you decide it's appropriate, share a selection with someone else. Your spouse. Your partner . . . friend . . . sex pal . . . parent . . . child . . . sibling . . . life coach . . . doctor . . . spiritual guide . . . therapist.

You are invited to post your responses on the blog

www.jeff devore1.wordpress.com

for the world to read . . . benefit from . . . laugh with you . . . rejoice with you . . . cry with you . . . sigh in relief with you . . . "I thought I was the only one . . ."

You have a message that may benefit others. A message you wish you had been told.

This is your Journal. It is your servant. Use it to express and possibly share your truth, from your perspective as the expert that you are.

About sex.

Your sex.

Thank You,
Jeff DeVore

Sex as . . .

. . . acceptance

Sex as . . .

. . . belonging

Sex as . . .

. . . caring

Sex as . . .

. . . connection

Sex as . . .

. . . shared

Sex as . . .

. . . love

Sex as . . .

. . . sparkling

Sex as . . .

. . . bargaining

Sex as . . .

. . . invitation

Sex as . . .

. . . functional

Sex as . . .

. . . energizing

Sex as . . .

. . . supplication

Sex as . . .

. . . denial

Sex as . . .

. . . hidden

Sex as . . .

. . . requirement

Sex as . . .

. . . communication

Sex as . . .

. . . anger

Sex as . . .

. . . appreciation

Sex as . . .

...gentleness

Sex as . . .

. . . deception

Sex as . . .

. . . abandonment

Sex as . . .

. . . rescuer

Sex as . . .

...Art

Sex as . . .

. . . community

Sex as . . .

. . . bully

Sex as . . .

. . . frozen

.

Sex as . . .

. . . joy

Sex as . . .

. . . demeaning

Sex as . . .

. . . diversion

Sex as . . .

. . . dull

Sex as . . .

. . . creative

Sex as . . .

. . . taboo

Sex as . . .

. . . curiosity

Sex as . . .

. . . betrayal

Sex as . . .

. . . discreet

Sex as . . .

. . . correction

Sex as . . .

. . . provocative

Sex as . . .

. . . touch

Sex as . . .

. . . expressive

Sex as . . .

. . . faithfulness

Sex as . . .

. . . expectation

Sex as . . .

...growth

Sex as . . .

. . . pain

Sex as . . .

. . . goodness

Sex as . . .

. . . decline

Sex as . . .

. . . forgiveness

Sex as . . .

. . . shaming

Sex as . . .

. . . freedom

Sex as . . .

. . . depression

Sex as . . .

. . . happiness

Sex as . . .

. . . God

Sex as . . .

...Risky

Sex as . . .

. . . abused

Sex as . . .

. . . selfless

Sex as . . .

. . . fear

Sex as . . .

. . . kindness

Sex as . . .

. . . death

Sex as . . .

. . . demand

Sex as . . .

. . . non-judgmental

Sex as . . .

. . . patience

Sex as . . .

. . . kinky

Sex as . . .

. . . abuser

Sex as . . .

. . . plateau

Sex as . . .

. . . pleasure

Sex as . . .

. . . vulnerability

Sex as . . .

. . . manipulative

Sex as . . .

. . . power

Sex as . . .

. . . caress

Sex as . . .

. . . perverse

Sex as . . .

. . . private

Sex as . . .

. . . procreation

Sex as . . .

. . . animalistic

Sex as . . .

. . . healing

Sex as . . .

. . . anesthesia

Sex as . . .

. . . fun

Sex as . . .

. . . consensual

Sex as . . .

. . . pornographic

Sex as . . .

. . . health

Sex as . . .

. . . profane

Sex as . . .

. . . tender

Sex as . . .

. . . life

Sex as . . .

. . . punishment

Sex as . . .

. . . refined

Sex as . . .

...rape

Sex as . . .

. . . risky

Sex as . . .

. . . hilarity

Sex as . . .

... holiness

Sex as . . .

. . . ritual

Sex as . . .

. . . release

Sex as . . .

. . . resistance

Sex as . . .

. . . relief

Sex as . . .

. . . rejection

Sex as . . .

. . . sacred

Sex as . . .

. . . truth

Sex as . . .

. . . resentment

Sex as . . .

. . . renewal

Sex as . . .

. . . selfish

Sex as . . .

. . . peace

Sex as . . .

. . . rescued

Sex as . . .

. . . torment

Sex as . . .

. . . resourceful

205

Sex as . . .

. . . shameful

Sex as . . .

. . . safety

Sex as . . .

. . . victim

Sex as . . .

. . . security

Sex as . . .

. . . seductive

Sex as . . .

. . . self-control

Sex as . . .

. . . tease

Sex as . . .

. . . whole

Sex as . . .

. . . wholesome

Sex as . . .

_____ *(your choice)*

Sex as . . .

_____ _(your choice)_

Sex as . . .

_____ (your choice)

Sex as . . .

_____ (your choice)

Sex as . . .

_____ (your choice)

Index

www.ingramcontent.com/pod-product-compliance
Lightning Source LLC
Chambersburg PA
CBHW021440070526
44577CB00002B/233